Legend
OF THE GOURD

Adapted and illustrated by Caren Ke'ala Loebel-Fried

Hawaiian translation by Kaliko Beamer-Trapp

Native Hawaiian Culture and Arts Program

Ua lehulehu a manomano ka 'ikena a ka Hawai'i.
Great and numerous is the knowledge of the Hawaiians.
—'Ōlelo No'eau 2814

This project is funded under the Native Hawaiian Culture and Arts Program in celebration of the Legacy of Excellence of Native Hawaiian culture. The Legacy of Excellence volumes are devoted to generating an appreciation of Native Hawaiian traditions, art, and language through education, awareness, and recognition of excellence in Native Hawaiian achievement.

The views and conclusions contained in this document are those of the authors and should not be interpreted as representing the opinions or policies of the U.S. Government. Mention of trade names or commercial products does not constitute their endorsement by the U.S. Government.

KAMAHOI
PRESS

Kamahoi Press is an imprint of the Bishop Museum Press.

Bishop Museum Press
1525 Bernice Street
Honolulu, Hawai'i 96817
www.bishopmuseum.org/press

ISBN: 978-1-58178-103-8

Design by Nancy Watanabe

Printed in China

Library of Congress Cataloging-in-Publication Data

Loebel-Fried, Caren.
  Legend of the gourd / adapted and illustrated by Caren Ke'ala Loebel-Fried ; Hawaiian translation by Kaliko Beamer-Trapp.
    p. cm.
  Includes bibliographical references (p.).
  ISBN 978-1-58178-103-8 (hardcover : alk. paper)
  [1. Hawaii--Folklore. 2. Hawaiian language materials--Bilingual.] I. Beamer-Trapp, Kaliko. II. Title.
  PZ90.H27L63 2010
  398.209969--dc22

          2010031891

Ahia la anoano a ke ahi-kanu, a kanu la, i pua i Hawaii? A kanu la o ka ipu nei; a ulu; a lau; a pua; a hua la o ka ipu nei.

How many seeds have been planted on the field cleared by fire to flourish in Hawaii? Planted is the gourd; it grows; it leafs; it blossoms; it bears fruit.

—A section of the "Pule Ipu," as written in David Malo's *Hawaiian Antiquities* English translation by Mary Kawena Pukui from *Native Planters in Old Hawaii*

Dedicated to my mom, who planted the original seed; my husband, whose vine path I share; my son, who inspires with his flowering and fruiting; and my friend Mary, who knows how to test for ripeness.

*L*ong ago in Ka'ū, Hawai'i, there lived a young man and woman who loved each other very much. Although they were both from families of *ali'i*, or chiefs, their parents did not approve of the relationship. And so they met in secret and talked about their hopes and dreams. One night after darkness fell, they ran away together.

'*O* Ka'ū, Hawai'i ka 'āina.
He mau 'ohana ali'i ko Ka'ū i ka wā kahiko, a no 'elua pua ali'i ho'i kēia mo'olelo: he kāne a he wahine 'ōpiopio. Ua nui ko lāua nei aloha kekahi i kekahi, akā 'a'ole i 'āpono mai nā 'ohana o lāua i ka pilina. Hui malū lāua a ho'olālā no ka wā e hiki mai ana. I ka pō 'ana mai o kekahi ahiahi, ha'alele malū ua mau liko ali'i 'elua nei.

There were many from the community who loved the young couple and decided to follow and help them. And so, on becoming man and wife, the couple also came to be chief and chiefess to these people. The group walked for many days on the sunny Kamāʻoa Plain, along the flank of Mauna Loa, on a journey to a new life.

Hahai maila ka poʻe i aloha a minamina iā lāua. I ke au o ka manawa, lilo lāua nei i aliʻi kāne a i aliʻi wahine hoʻi no lākou. Huakaʻi hele lākou a pau i ke kula makani nui o Kamāʻoa, ma ka umauma ākea hoʻi o Mauna Loa, e ʻimi aku ana i wahi e noho pū ai.

One day at sunset, the chief saw on the horizon a group of rising stars called *Huhui* (Pleiades). He knew the stormy season would soon arrive. He said, "Let us settle here near the shore, where we can gather food from the sea." Amid the swirling winds, they built huts to shelter themselves.

Iā lākou e haele ana, ʻike ʻia nā maka ʻōlinolino o nā hōkū ʻehiku ʻo Huihui ma ke ʻalihilani i ke ahiahi. He ʻōuli ia no ka hiki ʻana mai o ka wā hoʻoilo. ʻĪ maila ke aliʻi i ka poʻe, "E unoho ana kākou i kula kai. Ma ʻaneʻi e ola ai i ka iʻa a me ka ʻai." Kūkulu ʻia ihola kauhale nui kahi e noho ai.

Then came a time of winds from the south that brought drenching rain and loud, booming thunder. Waves pounded against the lava walls at the shore. Rain soaked the Kamāʻoa Plain. The people were happy, for the land would soon be ready to plant with seeds for food. And when it became known that the chiefess was *hāpai*, pregnant, the people were filled with joy.

Pā maila ka makani Kona, a ua mai ka ua o ka lani ʻIkuā. Kuʻi ka leo o ka hekili i loko o nā ao polohiwa o ka lewa. Kani hoʻi ka leo o nā nalu nui ma nā pali kuʻi o kai. Pulu ko Kamāʻoa i ka ua nui. Hauʻoli naʻe ka poʻe, no ka mea, e hiki mai ana ka wā e kanu ʻia ai ka ʻai. Pālua ka hauʻoli o ka poʻe i ka lohe ē, ua hāpai ke aliʻi wahine.

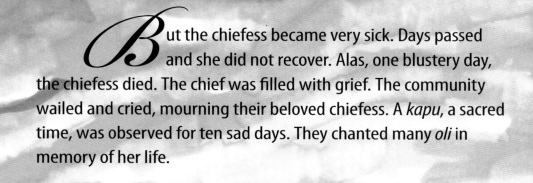

But the chiefess became very sick. Days passed and she did not recover. Alas, one blustery day, the chiefess died. The chief was filled with grief. The community wailed and cried, mourning their beloved chiefess. A *kapu*, a sacred time, was observed for ten sad days. They chanted many *oli* in memory of her life.

Maʻi ihola nō naʻe ke aliʻi wahine. ʻAʻole i polapola iki mai. ʻAʻole hoʻi i liʻuliʻu, a hoʻi akula i ke ala o nā kūpuna o ka pō. Luʻuluʻu loa ke aliʻi, a kūmākena hoʻi nā makaʻāinana me ka uē aloha nui. Ua kau ke kapu a hala ke anahulu—he ʻumi pō. Nui nā kanikau no ke aliʻi wahine i haʻalele akula.

As was the custom in the days of old Hawai'i, the chief found a cave hidden in the forest. He cleaned the cave and spread layers of fine *lauhala* matting on a shelf along the back wall. One clear night after the period of *kapu*, he secretly carried his wife's body to the cave. He lovingly laid her on the shelf and covered her with fine *kapa* sheets. Before her, he placed containers filled with young leaves from taro and sweet potato plants, *lū'au* and *palula*, her favorite foods.

Outside, he piled up stones to cover the entire entrance to the cave. It was crucial no one be able to find the body of the chiefess as her bones were sacred.

Huli akula ke ali'i i ana kūpono i ka wao o uka, kahi e waiho 'ia ai ke kino kupapa'u o kāna wahine. Ho'oma'ema'e 'o ia iā loko a hohola i ka moena makali'i ma ka paepae pōhaku o loko loa. I ka hopena o ka wā kapu ma ia hope iho, hūnā ihola 'o ia i ke kino wailua i ke ana a wahī i ke kapa a me ke kilohana nani. Waiho pū 'ia he mau 'umeke a me nā ho'okupu i piha i ka mea'ai punahele a ka wahine: 'o ka lū'au, a me ka palula ho'i.

Ho'āhu ke ali'i i nā pōhaku ma waho o ke ana i hiki 'ole i ka po'e ke komo i loko. Pa'a ihola.

Many weeks passed. One night the people heard strange and mournful cries coming from the sky. They all knew it was 'Ewe'ewe-iki, the famous ghost mother who died in childbirth with her spirit baby. No one was afraid of the ghost mother, for she was a part of life in Ka'ū. Whenever a woman was ready to give birth, 'Ewe'ewe-iki would fly over her house the night before the baby was to be born. But when the people heard her cries that night, they looked at each other in surprise, for no one in the community was expecting a baby.

He mahina ma hope mai, lohe nā maka'āinana i ka leo pānewanewa o 'Ewe'eweiki i ka pō. 'O ia ka 'uhane lele o ka wahine kahiko i hala i ka wā e hānau 'ia mai ana kāna keiki, a ma'a ko Ka'ū i kāna uē. Ke kokoke mai ka hānau 'ana o kekahi makuahine, lele 'o 'Ewe'eweiki me kāna keiki 'uhane i luna o ka hale kahi e hānau ai, a kūkala i ka mea hou. 'A'ole i maka'u ka po'e i ka lohe 'ana i kāna uē; he pū'iwa na'e 'oiai 'a'ohe wahine i kokoke i ka hānau i ia manawa.

The next day in the dark burial cave, a tiny vine sprouted from the *piko*, the navel, of the chiefess. The vine meandered across the floor and up the wall of the musty cave, drawn to a beam of light piercing through a crack in the ceiling. The vine curled its way right through the crack, emerging into a fresh Kamāʻoa rain-shower.

I ia lā ma hope mai, i loko lilo hoʻi o ke ana kahi o ke kino wailua o ke aliʻi wahine e waiho ana, kupu mai kahi muʻo liʻiliʻi mai loko aʻe o kona piko, a kā aku hoʻi a piʻi ma ka ʻaoʻao a i luna loa i kahi o ka mālamalama o ka lā e makili mai ana. Piʻi aʻela ke kā e huli ana i ka lani o luna, a puka maila i ke ao ma ka ua hoʻoilo o Kamāʻoa.

The little green vine crept through the forest, growing thicker each day. Leaves sprouted from the left and right sides of its stem. Its tendrils reached out to grab onto roots and small *moa* and *'ala 'ala wai nui* plants growing at the base of trees. The sturdy vine snaked its way out onto the plain and its tendrils clung to ruts in the *pāhoehoe* lava. Like tiny fingers, the tendrils wrapped themselves tightly around jutting lava rocks and clumps of *pili* grasses.

Kōkolo akula hoʻi ke kā i ka nahele a laumanamana ma kēlā ʻaoʻao, kēia ʻaoʻao: hihihi aʻela nā ʻaweʻawe i ka moa a me ka ʻalaʻalawainui e ulu ana ma lalo o nā kumulāʻau. Hoʻomau akula a hiki i ka pāhoehoe o ke kula o Kamāʻoa kai. Kōʻaiʻai nā ʻaweʻawe i ke kumu o ke pili a ma nā kiokio pōhaku a paʻa.

$\mathcal{A}$ll through the season of storms the vine traveled up the coast of Ka'ū, its leaves flapping and fluttering in the wind and rain, but the vine held itself firmly in place. Over miles and miles of the rolling Kamā'oa Plain the vine travelled across many *ahupua'a*. From its source in the cave at Kamā'oa, it grew through Pākini-iki, Pākini-nui, and Kahuku. It crept through the tiny district of Kī'ao, and then through the larger district of Manukā.

$\mathcal{K}$ikī holo akula ma ka lihi 'ōpalipali o Ka'ū. E kāwelowelo kapalili ana nā lau i ka makani a me ka ua, pa'a nō na'e nā a'a kolo i ka honua. Kokolo aku ho'i a hala nā ahupua'a i kapa 'ia i kēia mau lā 'o Pākininui, Pākiniiki, Kahuku, Kī'ao, a me ke ahupua'a nui 'o Manukā.

And then, finally, just after it crossed the border of Kona into Kapu'a, from the end of the vine sprouted a white blossom.

The winds were changing, going this way and that, and a sudden gust threatened to tear the tender blossom right off the vine. But the flower held on, its petals doing a wild dance. The sun peeked out from behind the clouds and shined brightly on the white blossom.

A ma ka hiki loa 'ana aku i ke ahupua'a 'o Kapu'a, pua maila ma ka welelau. He pua ke'oke'o a lahilahi.

'Ānihaniha nō a hemo ka pua i ka makani nui o ia 'āina. Ua pa'a na'e i ke kumu. Pā maila ka lā i kona mau lihilihi e ha'a ana i 'ō i 'ane'i.

After a time, the flower withered and the wind swept it away. And there on the vine where the flower had been was a tiny green gourd. The baby gourd lay in the shade of its leaves, its skin covered with a soft layer of downy hairs.

Ike au o ka manawa, mae ka pua a lawe ʻia aʻela na ka makani. Ma kahi naʻe o ka pua e ulu ana ma mua, hua maila he wahi ipu liʻiliʻi a ʻōmaʻomaʻo nona ka heuheu palupalu loa. Hoʻopūnana ʻia ma nā lau e ulu mai ana a puni.

$\mathcal{W}$inter had passed and the sun shone full and bright on the land. The heat from the sun helped the gourd grow a little bigger every day. Soon the soft downy hairs were rubbed off by the gourd's leaves flapping against it. Now its green skin had white patches, so it blended perfectly with the sun dappled leaves around it.

On a lava ridge just above where the small gourd grew, there stood the hut of a fisherman. The time for good fishing had arrived and as the fisherman stood outside his hut scanning the sea, he saw something curious on the rolling plains below.

$\mathcal{H}$ala ihola ka wā hoʻoilo. Emi ka hua, a nui maila ka ipu liʻiliʻi. Pā mai ka lā a wela ke kula. Hemo ka heuheu i ke kūlepe mau o nā lau i ka ʻili, a pāniʻoniʻo hoʻi ka ʻili i ka ʻōmaʻomaʻo a me ke keʻokeʻo, e like hoʻi me nā lau i ka lā ke nānā aku.

Aia kokoke mai he pāpaʻi lawaiʻa. Ua hiki mai ka wā o ka makahiki no ka lawaiʻa ʻana, a kū ka lawaiʻa ma waho o kona hale e kilo mai ana i nā ʻōuli o ka lani a me ke kai. I kona ʻalawa ʻana i ke kula maloʻo o kai, ʻike ʻo ia i ka mea ʻano ʻē ma laila. Iho ʻo ia e nānā.

When he went down to investigate, he discovered the gourd. "Ah, look at this!" he exclaimed, "What a fine gourd! When it grows big, I can use it as an *ipu holoholona* to store my fishing gear!" He grabbed handfuls of *pili* grasses growing nearby and piled them underneath the gourd, setting it upright so it would grow round and not flat on one side.

The next day, he built a frame over the gourd with three sticks. Carefully lifting the gourd by its vine, he suspended it from the frame, and then removed all the tiny stones from the ground beneath it. He checked the gourd every day and marveled at how big and fat it grew. Weeks passed and one day as the fisherman examined the stem, he noticed it had started to wither. He squeezed and thumped the gourd, testing it for ripeness. But it was not yet ready to be harvested.

Akahi o ua ipu liʻiliʻi nei, kāhāhā maila ʻo ia, "'Ā! He aha lā hoʻi kēia?" Hāhā a milimili ʻo ia i ia mea haʻohaʻo. "He wahi mea kupanaha hoʻi. Ke nui aʻe, he kūpono ana nō paha i wahi ipu holoholona naʻu!" E noʻonoʻo ana i kāna mau pono lawaiʻa hoʻi. ʻOhi ʻo ia i ke pili e ulu kokoke mai ana, a hana ihola i wahi palupalu e noho ai ka ipu a poepoe pono ke kino ke ulu aʻe. ʻAʻole maikaʻi ke pālahalaha kekahi ʻaoʻao.

Kāpili pū hoʻi ʻo ia i haka lāʻau e lewa ai ka ipu. I kēlā lā kēia lā, hele mai ʻo ia e mālama i ka ipu. Hauʻoli ʻo ia i ka holokū o ke kino, ʻo ia hoʻi ke kino poepoe nani ke nānā aku. He mau anahulu ma hope mai, maloʻo mai ke kano e pili ai ka ipu i ke kā. ʻIniki a kīkēkē ka lawaiʻa i ke kino, i mea e ʻike ai inā paha ua oʻo a mākaukau. ʻAʻole naʻe i kāhala i ia manawa.

That night, back in Kamāʻoa, the chiefess visited her husband in a dream. She cried to him, "Auwe! Auwe! I am sore and bruised!" The chief awoke abruptly, startled by the dream. In the early morning light, he rushed to the burial cave and tore through the rocks at the entrance, stumbling inside toward his wife's body. He stopped short before her. In the dim light of the cave, he saw the vine.

I ia pō hoʻokahi nō, ʻōʻili ka ʻuhane o ke aliʻi wahine ma ka hale o ke aliʻi ma Kamāʻoa. E uē mai ana ka wahine. "Auī! Auī hoʻi! ʻEha koʻu ʻōpū!" Hikilele ke aliʻi, he moeʻuhane kā! Pupuʻu hoʻolei loa ʻo ia i ka nahele ʻoi wanaʻao a wehewehe i nā pōhaku i paʻa ai ka ʻīpuka komo o ke ana, huli ʻo ia i ke kino o kāna wahine i hala. He pūʻiwa honua naʻe i ka ʻike ʻana ē he lāʻau hihi e ulu ana mai ka piko aʻe.

He ran out of the cave and followed the vine along its winding path through the forest and out onto the Kamā'oa Plain. In the morning sunshine, he crouched to examine the thick, ribbed vine, marveling at how the tendrils clung so firmly to cracks in the lava. Like little grasping fingers, the tiny tendrils held the vine down so tight that the chief could barely lift it off the ground.

Ho'okolo akula ke ali'i i kahi o ka lā'au i ulu kolo aku ai. Ho'okolo ho'i ma ka nahele, a kakahiaka maila, aia i ke kula malo'o 'o Kamā'oa i kai. Ha'oha'o ka mana'o o ke ali'i i ka nani o ia wahi lā'au uaua: i ke kā mānoanoa a hālu'a, a i nā 'ōka'i e wili ana a pa'a pono mā nā māwae o ka papa pāhoehoe.

Clouds layered the horizon. The wind pushed him, and the vine leaves waved him on. And so he followed the vine through the day across the Kamā'oa Plain. As night fell, the vine led the chief into a shallow valley that was sheltered from the wind. He lay down next to the vine and touched it tenderly. And then he slept. In the morning, the wind whistled in his ear to wake him. He rose, stretched, and began once again to follow the vine. The day was hot and windy, and the sun pounded on his head. The chief wondered if the vine would ever end. Exhausted, he asked, "Where are you leading me, my dear wife?"

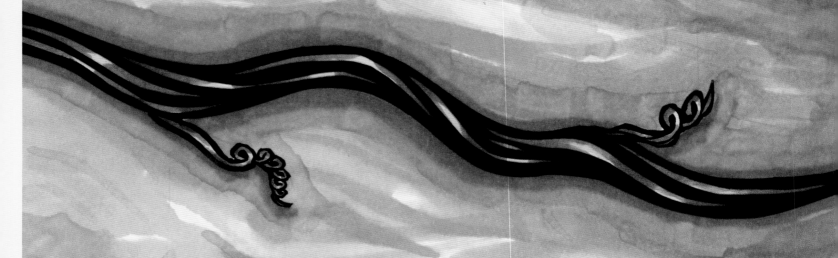

Nui nā 'ōpua o ka lewa, pā ka makani, a kani ke pola o ka malo i ka holo 'ana o ke ali'i. Lō'ihi ka ho'okolo 'ana i ka lā'au, a ahiahi ihola, hō'ea loa aku i kahi ihona 'āina i malu i ka makani 'ole. Hō'aumoe 'o ia ma kahi o ke kā e moe ana i ka honua a wana'ao maila. Na ka leo o ke aheahe lau makani i ho'āla mai i ke ali'i me he mele ho'āla la ia. Kū a'ela 'o ia a ho'omālō i kona kino ma'e'ele. Ho'okolo hou aku i kahi o ka lā'au i ulu ai. 'Ena ka lā i ka hokua, a 'eha ho'i kona po'o. 'Ainea a luhi hewa ho'i ke ali'i. Ui akula 'o ia i ka lā'au, "I hea lā ho'i kāua e la'i ai, e ku'u wahine?"

And then he saw the gourd. He ran to the gourd and swept it up into his arms. He cradled it like a baby, joyfully rocking it back and forth.

A ma ia wā ho'okahi nō, 'ike ihola 'o ia i ka ipu. Holo aku 'o ia a lālau mai i ka ipu. Hi'i 'o ia ma kona poli, me he keiki lā ke hi'ilei 'ia mai.

Just then the fisherman spied the stranger holding the gourd. He rushed out shouting, "Let go of that gourd! It belongs to me!" The chief tried to explain about his wife and the dream, but the fisherman would not listen. They argued until finally the fisherman agreed to follow the chief to the source of the gourd vine. It was only after they entered the burial cave that the fisherman understood and relented. He wished the chief well.

'Oiai he maka kilo ko ka lawai'a, 'ike koke 'o ia i ke ali'i e hi'i ana i kāna ipu. Holo akula 'o ia me ka 'uā 'ana aku, "'Eā! Na'u kēnā wahi ipu kekela! E ho'oku'u 'ia!" Haha'i maila ke ali'i i ka mo'olelo no kāna wahine a no ka moe'uhane, 'a'ole na'e i maliu iki ka lawai'a. Ho'opa'apa'a aku, ho'opa'apa'a mai lāua. Ho'oholo ho'i lāua e uhele like i ke ana. I ka 'ike maka 'ana o ka lawai'a i ka piko, ho'oku'u 'o ia i kona huoi 'awa'awa, a waipahē maila kona 'ano.

Night was falling. The chief brought the gourd home and gently wrapped it in many layers of soft *kapa* cloth. He rested it on a pile of *lauhala* matting. The next morning, when he unwrapped the *kapa*, he discovered that the gourd had cracked. He carefully pulled the gourd open, and into his palms fell two seeds.

The chief cupped the seeds in his hands and looked at them with wonder. He knew that these seeds would provide many useful gourds for his people. "Thank you, dear wife," he whispered. Then, suddenly, the seeds began to grow. Two warm soft fruits covered with downy hairs quickly filled his hands.

Hoʻihoʻi ke aliʻi i ka ipu i kona hale, wahī i ke kapa paʻūpaʻū palupalu loa, a waiho ma ka moena lau hala. Ma ia kakahiaka mai, wehe aʻela ʻo ia i ke kapa a pūʻiwa loa maila nō: ua mahae lua ka ipu! Wehe mai ke aliʻi i nā hapa ʻelua o ka ipu a hāʻule maila ʻelua ʻanoʻano ma kona poho lima.

They grew bigger, sprouting arms and legs, and before long he held in his arms two baby girls. He joyfully hugged the twins and they giggled, each grabbing one of his fingers. Their tiny fingers held on so tightly, the chief remembered the tendrils of the gourd vine. He knew these girls would be strong and that they would grow up with firm ties to their people and their land.

The chief introduced the twins of the gourd to his people and they loved the daughters born from their beloved chief and chiefess. They helped raise the two children and taught them the ways of their people.

Ulu aʻe ia mau ʻanoʻano, a kino maila, he ʻelua kaikamahine ia e minoʻaka mai ana i ka makua ʻo ke aliʻi. Pūʻili ikaika nā lima liʻiliʻi o nā keiki i ka manamana o ka makua e like me ka ikaika o nā maʻawe o ka ipu i ka honua. ʻIke ke aliʻi ē, e noho ana a kupa kēia mau māhoe i ka ʻāina.

Launa ua mau māhoe lā a ka ipu i ka poʻe pili mai, a aloha nui ʻia lāua ʻoiai he mau keiki na nā aliʻi ʻelua mai. Hānai ʻia a nui e like me ke ʻano kuʻuna o ia mau wahi.

And so the twins grew to be powerful women and great warriors who had many children of their own. The years and generations followed and the twins of the gourd became ancestors to many people.

Like the gourd vine, the family spread and settled all over the Kamāʻoa Plain. Near the shore lived fishermen, in the valleys and up the slopes of Mauna Loa lived farmers. The fishermen and farmers traded and shared food from the land and the sea. Soon descendants of the twins numbered in the thousands.

And the people called themselves, "The Children of the Gourd."

Nui hou aʻe nā māhoe ʻelua a kanakamakua, a lilo he mau kūpuna no nā hanauna ma hope mai.

E like hoʻi me ka laha ʻana aʻe o ka ipu ʻawaʻawa ma ka ʻāina, pēia ka laha o ka ʻohana ma Kamāʻoa mā. Noho aku nā lawaiʻa i kahakai a noho mai nā mahiʻai i ka wao kanaka o uka. Kūʻai kaʻana aku, kūʻai kaʻana mai ka poʻe i ka iʻa a me ka ʻai a ola aʻe kānaka a māhuahua ka ʻāina i nā mamo he mau lau ka nui.

A pēlā i kapa ʻia ai ka inoa o ka poʻe o Kamāʻoa mā ʻo "Nā Mamo a ka Ipu ʻAwaʻawa."

Afterword

He ipu nui!	A huge ipu!
O hiki ku mauna	Growing like a mountain
O hiki kua	To be carried on the back
Nui maoli keia ipu!	Really huge is this gourd!

The *ipu*, the gourd, was one of the most important and beloved of plants in ancient Hawai'i. A symbol of abundance, with its round and full shape, the *ipu* was one of the body forms of Lono the Provider, a nourishing god associated with rain clouds, plant growth, and the harvest.

Many types of gourds were cultivated and grew in various shapes and sizes with different uses. Used as containers for food, fishing gear, or *kapa* (cloth), gourds also helped to collect and contain water, a necessity on the dry Kamā'oa Plain.

For those on the Kamā'oa Plain, the *ipu* was considered an ancestor. A gourd would be placed by the head of a woman during a difficult birth so the ancestor could help with the delivery. The *ipu 'awa'awa* type, especially, was cared for like a child—tended throughout its growing, blossoming, and fruiting periods. When the young fruit appeared, it was nurtured, protected, and watched closely, until it was ready to pick and be dried. To keep others from stealing a prized gourd growing on the vine, it would be given an ancestor's name.

Like a womb, the gourd contained the seeds of life. In this legend, as the gourd vine spread its tendrils throughout the Kamā'oa Plain, so too did the chiefly lines of the people populate the land in the days of ancient Hawai'i.

Sources

Handy, E.S. Craighill, Elisabeth G. Handy, & Mary Kawena Pukui. 1972. *Native Planters in Old Hawaii: Their Life, Lore, and Environment.* Bernice P. Bishop Museum Bulletin 233. Honolulu: Bishop Museum Press.

Handy, E.S. Craighill, & Mary Kawena Pukui. 1958. *The Polynesian Family System in Ka-'u, Hawai'i.* Rutland, Vermont: Charles E. Tuttle.

Kamali, Keliihue. 1935. "The people of Kamaoa, Ka'ū. Legend of a Gourd." Hawaiian Ethnographical Notes #1099. Bishop Museum Library Archives, Honolulu.

Pukui, Mary Kawena. 1942. *Hawaiian Beliefs and Customs During Birth, Infancy, and Childhood.* Occasional Papers of Bernice P. Bishop Museum, vol. XVI, no. 17. Honolulu: Bishop Museum Press.

About the Art

The art in this book is made with hand-colored block prints. The technique is similar to Hawaiian *'ohe kāpala*. In ancient times, women carved patterns into strips cut from the inside bark of bamboo plants. The bamboo "stamps" were dipped into natural dyes and pressed onto bark cloth in repeating patterns. The prints in this book are made from rubber block prints, printed with black ink, and then painted with washes of colored inks.